Earth Basics

Water

by Rebecca Pettiford

Bullfrog Books

Ideas for Parents and Teachers

Bullfrog Books let children practice reading informational text at the earliest reading levels. Repetition, familiar words, and photo labels support early readers.

Before Reading

- Discuss the cover photo. What does it tell them?
- Look at the picture glossary together. Read and discuss the words.

Read the Book

- "Walk" through the book and look at the photos. Let the child ask questions. Point out the photo labels.
- Read the book to the child, or have him or her read independently.

After Reading

- Prompt the child to think more. Ask: Water comes in three different forms. One form is frozen, as ice. Have you seen frozen water? Where was it?

Bullfrog Books are published by Jump!
5357 Penn Avenue South
Minneapolis, MN 55419
www.jumplibrary.com

Copyright © 2024 Jump! International copyright reserved in all countries. No part of this book may be reproduced in any form without written permission from the publisher.

Library of Congress Cataloging-in-Publication Data

Names: Pettiford, Rebecca, author.
Title: Water / by Rebecca Pettiford.
Description: Minneapolis, MN: Jump!, Inc. [2024]
Series: Earth basics | Includes index.
Audience: Ages 5–8
Identifiers: LCCN 2022045819 (print)
LCCN 2022045820 (ebook)
ISBN 9798885244480 (hardcover)
ISBN 9798885244497 (paperback)
ISBN 9798885244503 (ebook)
Subjects: LCSH: Water—Juvenile literature.
Classification: LCC GB671 .P37 2024 (print)
LCC GB671 (ebook)
DDC 551.48—dc23/eng20230111
LC record available at https://lccn.loc.gov/2022045819
LC ebook record available at https://lccn.loc.gov/2022045820

Editor: Katie Chanez
Designer: Emma Almgren-Bersie

Photo Credits: CK Foto/Shutterstock, cover; Damsea/Shutterstock, 1; Delbars/Shutterstock, 3; Gorynvd/Shutterstock, 4; Artsiom P/Shutterstock, 5 (Earth); Steven's Light/Shutterstock, 5 (background); Gestalt Imagery/Shutterstock, 6–7 (top), 23bm; Ruslan Suseynov/Shutterstock, 6–7 (bottom); Jurjanephoto/Shutterstock, 8–9, 23tr; Senya and Ksusha/Shutterstock, 10–11, 23br; TWStock/Shutterstock, 12; Evgeny Atamanenko/Shutterstock, 13; Koldunov Alexey/Shutterstock, 14–15; amenic181/Shutterstock, 16; Hendrik Martens/Shutterstock, 17; Robbi Akbari Kamaruddin/Alamy, 18–19; FamVeld/Shutterstock, 20–21; stockelements/Shutterstock, 22 (top); Yevhenii Chulovskyi/Shutterstock, 22ml; Gcapture/Shutterstock, 22mr; railway fx/Shutterstock, 22bl; Kay Cee Lens and Footages/Shutterstock, 22br; Farik gallery/Shutterstock, 23tl; xpixel/Shutterstock, 23tm; Matis75/Shutterstock, 23bl; K.-U. Haessler/Shutterstock, 24.

Printed in the United States of America at Corporate Graphics in North Mankato, Minnesota.

Table of Contents

Always Moving 4
The Water Cycle 22
Picture Glossary 23
Index 24
To Learn More 24

Always Moving

Ben is thirsty.

He drinks water.

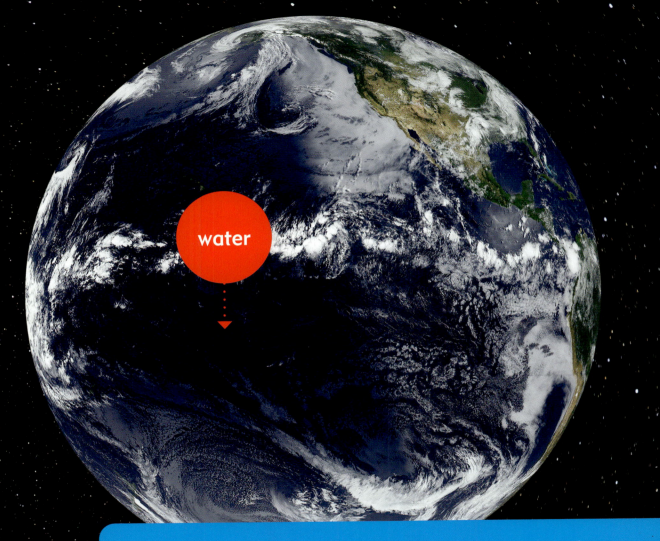

Water covers most of Earth.

Water shapes Earth.
How?
Rivers flow.
Waves crash.

Water is not always a liquid.

It can freeze.

Then it is ice.

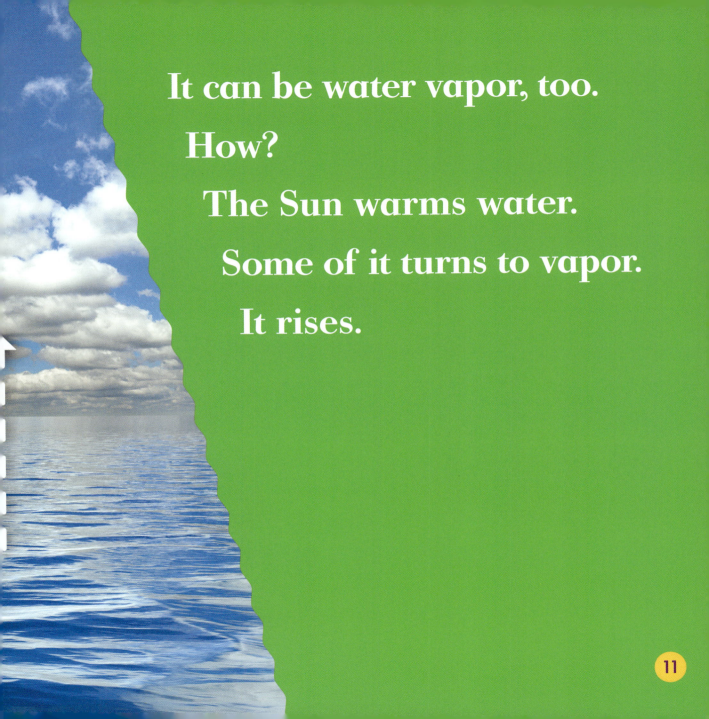

It can be water vapor, too.
How?
The Sun warms water.
Some of it turns to vapor.
It rises.

It mixes with dust in the air.
Clouds form.

Vapor cools.
It falls as rain.

Rain lands in lakes and rivers.

It lands in oceans, too.

The cycle starts again.

Plants need water to grow.

Animals need water to live. Some live in it.

fish

We need water to live, too.

We drink it.

We cook and wash with it.

It is hot.

Let's swim in the water!

The Water Cycle

The water cycle is the path water takes as it moves around Earth. What are the steps in the water cycle? Take a look!

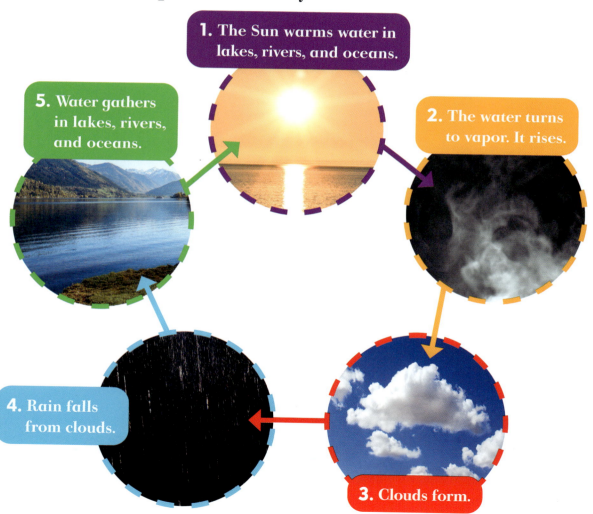

1. The Sun warms water in lakes, rivers, and oceans.
2. The water turns to vapor. It rises.
3. Clouds form.
4. Rain falls from clouds.
5. Water gathers in lakes, rivers, and oceans.

Picture Glossary

cycle
A set of actions that happens again and again in the same order.

dust
Tiny particles of dirt that gather on surfaces or float in air.

freeze
To become solid or turn into ice at a very low temperature.

liquid
Something that flows and can be poured.

shapes
Molds, carves, or determines how something will form.

water vapor
A gas made of drops of water mixed with air.

Index

animals 17
clouds 12
Earth 5, 7
ice 8
lakes 14
liquid 8
oceans 14
plants 16
rain 13, 14
rivers 7, 14
Sun 11
water vapor 11, 13

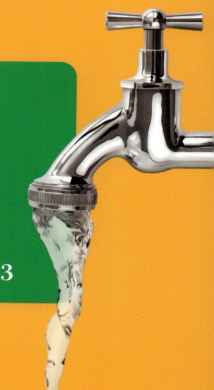

To Learn More

Finding more information is as easy as 1, 2, 3.
❶ Go to www.factsurfer.com
❷ Enter "water" into the search box.
❸ Choose your book to see a list of websites.